the
logic
of
whistling

Also by Richard Skinner

Leaping & Staggering (Dilettante, 1988/1996)
In The Stillness: a sequence of poems based on Julian of Norwich (Dilettante, 1990)
The Melting Woman (Blue Button, 1993)
Still Staggering… (Dilettante, 1995)
Echoes of Eckhart (Arthur James, 1998)

———

the
logic
of
whistling

Richard Skinner

CAIRNS PUBLICATIONS

HARLECH

2002

British Library Cataloguing in Publication Data:
A record for this book is available from the British Library

ISBN 1 870652 37 1

Cairns Publications
Dwylan, Stryd Fawr, Harlech, Gwynedd LL46 2YA

www.cottercairns.co.uk
office@cottercairns.co.uk – orders
jim@cottercairns.co.uk – editorial

Typeset in Monotype Columbus by
Strathmore Publishing Services, London EC1

Printed in Great Britain by
Stanley L. Hunt, Rushden

Contents

Probes   1

The Gods of Old   3
After the Catastrophe   4
The Task   5
Heresy   6
Against the Odds   7
Seams   8
Other   9
Blizzard   10
Ideas   11
The Look   12
Equivalent   13
Two Questions   14
The Mesh   15
The Eighth Deadly Sin   16
The Challenge   17
Winner   18
Probes   19
Honey   20

Dancing the Ultra-Violet   21

The First Haiku of Spring   23
The Flexible Liner   24
The Garden Pond (I)   25
The Garden Pond (II)   26
Between Worlds   27
The Old Fence   28
Cabbage White   29
Swallows   30
Detachment   31
Waiting for Angels   32
At Woodbury Castle   33

Sonnet to the River Otter   34
The Quarry   35
The Falcon Sonnets   36

Had We Your Gifts   **39**
The Logic of Whistling   41
Lacking the Latin   42
Caravaggio's 'The Fortune-Teller'   44
Vincent's Chair with Pipe   45
At 'The Art of Holy Russia'   46
If My Father Were to See the Work
    of Rachel Whiteread   47
Presto   48
Of Sheep and Goats   49
The Second Part   50

In the Lines of Your Face   **53**
Christmas Card   55
Couple Therapy   57
At the Sea   58
Brave for a Moment   59
Sophia   61
Family Funeral   62
To Solitude   63

The Gap   **69**
Ten Speculations on Michelangelo's
    The Creation of Adam   71

Alas   **81**
Abraham and God at the Gates of Sodom   83

Acknowledgements

At Woodbury Castle, The Quarry and *Sonnet to the River Otter* were written as part of a commission from East Devon Council.

The Falcon Sonnets were first published in *Still Staggering...* (Dilettante, 1995).

The First Haiku of Spring were commissioned by Exeter Health Care Arts.

Lacking the Latin was a prize-winning poem in the 1998 "Write for Life" competition organised by Worthing Steyne Inner Wheel on behalf of the *Cancer Research Campaign.*

I am very grateful to a number of fellow poets, in particular Christopher Southgate, who have given much valuable response to work in progress over the years; and to Jim Cotter of Cairns Publications for his support and encouragement in bringing this book into being.

Probes

... For me now
there is only the God-space
into which I send out
my probes...

R. S. Thomas

When R. S. Thomas died in September 2000, I took down his *Collected Poems* and once again marvelled at his poetic explorations into, *inter alia*, faith, doubt, science and knowledge, and the interactions between them. I was stimulated to begin a fresh spell of writing myself, and the outcome is the following sequence which I would like to dedicate to him – although whether or not the fierce Welshman or his shade would accept a dedication from an Englishman is debatable.

The Gods of Old

We no longer pray to the bully
swaggering in the playground
while we cower in the toilets
fearing a bloody nose, a twisted arm;

nor to the sarcastic master
whose fine line in humiliation
and outbursts of anger
we anxiously seek to defuse;

nor to Judge Dredd nor the Terminator
nor the invading alien nor any of those
our insecurities could appropriate
to fashion into a fearsome God;

for we are grown-up now, know about
the psychology of projection,
the archetype of the Shadow,
how only fear itself is to be feared:

until, at three o'clock of a sleepless night,
like a river ripping from its channel
in flood, reclaiming its former course,
obliterating our hard-won territory,

the gods of old come rampaging back.

After the Catastrophe

Moving among the ruins, we think
we've spotted the figure of God,
but with our eyes still smarting
from all the acrid dust whirled up
by this catastrophe, we cannot be sure.

All we can be certain of is this:
the structure we elaborated
through untold years, brick by
philosophic brick, to span the chasm
between what is and what could be,
has just come crashing down.

The consequence of some crass flaw
in our design? The use of duff
materials? Miscalculation of
the total weight of expectations
the structure was to bear? Too soon
to say. No doubt a full enquiry will
help apportion blame…

                      We continue
picking through the rubble, and see
the figure moving off. Discover,
when he's gone, he's left behind
a trail of bread crumbs.

The Task

And God said
what do you make of this?
as the phenomena of experience
raw and unchecked
came tumbling about us
like an earthquaked house.

Our protestations
that we could make nothing
from rubble
being received in silence
we began our task
with curiosity our only tool.

Heresy

Since we had been
led to believe
how imperative it was
to recognize
the one true noun
which alone
could enlighten us
with its plenitude of meaning,
we sought this paragon
in all corners
of the language,
investigating every clause
and parenthesis,
interrogating
every gathering of vocables;
but only countless pronouns
presented themselves,
until, unable to judge
the claim of each to be
the noun's sole representative,
we abandoned our quest,
choosing instead
to sit beside
a pool
of quiet reflection.
In its depths
we catch a glimpse
of a verb
gently
gliding.

Against the Odds

We have not for many years
sat at the gaming table
with the tweaker of the odds:
the one who ensured
we caught *this* bus,
met *that* girl,
responded to the sudden impulse
to buy a different paper and
spot the vital ad.

He tweaked his last in our world
when the bicycle pedal sheared
as the lorry overtook the young lad.
A freakish accident, according
to the papers.

No, he has lost
his loaded dice, his signs and portents,
all his tweaking paraphernalia.
He can only enter the game again
as the young lad, the lorry driver,
the manufacturer of bicycles;

or be the appalled onlooker.

Seams

We have been
working this seam for too long;
the quality of what we extract
has markedly diminished;
it neither feeds the fires
of our imagination nor quickens
the heart.

We have heard of
other seams, loaded (it is said)
with ore as rich in the Spirit
as any we have found, plunging
as deep (some would say deeper)
into the rock. Tempting
to try one.

We, however,
have been shaped by this seam,
are accustomed to its vagaries;
another seam would not be
our seam, would not accommodate
our contours; could well resist
the tools we have fashioned
over the centuries.

We resume
our tunnelling into the dark,
now with the suspicion it is we,
all along, who are the seam
being worked.

Other

"...all that I have written now seems like straw."
Thomas Aquinas

When we first encountered
the mysterious Other,
we lacked sufficient concepts
to understand our experience,
to encapsulate the significance
of disclosure.
Turning aside,
we devoted ourselves to shaping
an array of marvellous devices –
Hubble telescopes of the spirit,
cloud chambers of the soul –
with which to confirm or confute
our tentative hypotheses.

Our devices grew more marvellous,
our concepts more acute:
we returned to the Other intent
on using them to pierce the blaze
of its Otherness,
only to see
all we had fashioned consumed
as so much straw in a furnace.

Blizzard

If God were a natural phenomenon
I would nominate blizzard

for its ferocity
embodied in softness;

an obliteration of horizons
into which we are called

like so many Captain Oates
knowing that some time

is an eternity.

Ideas

Stepping back, God created
a vacuum into which
a multitude of ideas instantly
erupted, boiling furiously
in the absence of a countervailing
pressure.

        Many were ripped apart
by the initial frenzy, many more
survived the first few nanoseconds
only to perish in the succeeding phase
of fierce competition. Few made it
to maturity.

        Surveying the soup
of surviving ideas, God chose one,
placed it in a garden He had fashioned,
watched it curiously from behind
a tree. There

        it slithered and hissed
and was cunning.

The Look

God looked.

Conscious for the first time
of separation
we shuddered.

Should we retreat
or approach?

We looked
at one another,

absorbed ourselves briefly
as subjects being the object
of another's gaze.

Conscious for a second time
of separation
we clumsily embraced.

God chose that moment
to approach.

Equivalent

There are not many deserts
in this part of the world. We
are thus advised to seek out
a therapist to help us with
our inner desert (populated,
of course, by inner wild animals).

After the therapeutic equivalent
of forty days and forty nights
being tempted to turn our
inner stones to inner bread,
we feel ready to embark on
our life's mission. The bustle

of the market place overwhelms.

Two Questions

God stepped out
from His hiding place in
the scent of orange blossom
and looked around. He saw
in the bustle of human life
a mixture of fear and delight
He could not fully comprehend.

Tell me (catching hold of a
passer-by) what is it you fear?

What is it you most delight in?

Looking embarrassed, like
one who has just walked into
a plate-glass door, the woman
hurried away, turning the corner
without a second glance.

The Mesh

Since the given rules
did not fully fit
the given situation,

we requested their further
refinement, yielding a mesh
of ramifications. We hoped

the whole of ethical space
would thus be mapped,
leaving no interstices
of uncertainty. But

with every given refinement
the interstices multiplied,
and the finer the mesh became

the more we felt like
flies asking a spider
to spin a better web.

The Eighth Deadly Sin

I have given you, God said, one
for each day of the week, they
will surely suffice, there are
no others.
            But we continued to
importune Him, believing
He had kept the worst for Himself;
until, having shown us His
empty hands in vain, He caused
a deep sleep to engulf us…
                        Waking
to the dim light of a new dawn,
we felt a vague sense of guilt
for something the nature of which
still eludes us.

The Challenge

"… in poetry, one is wrestling with a god…"
Stephen Spender

God chose
not to respond, foreseeing
that to wrestle the challenger
would result in irrevocable
change.
Again the anguished plea,
again He chose to remain
hidden by the cloud of unknowing,
with only His evident absence
betraying His presence.

But the voice continued to demand
He reveal Himself, He commit
to a contest, that one might finally
overcome the other…
At last,
wearied by the importuning,
He parted the cloud, stepped out,
and faced the audacity
of Language…

A result is
yet to be announced.

Winner

It was not the Word
we had been expecting.

Love had been the front runner
closely followed by hope,
peace, mercy and grace.

Faith had been popular,
as had justice. Reward
also had its supporters.

Then God created laughter
and all bets were off.

Probes

My first, a christening present,
transmits on a single, fundamental
frequency. Although the clarity astonishes,
the content never varies and I
have long since stopped tuning in.
The transmissions continue nonetheless.

My second, which I launched
in my twenties, hurtles along
an unplottable course, liberally
transmitting on all possible frequencies:
a marvellous cacophony which
I am still hoping to translate.

Transmissions from my third,
dispatched ten years ago, mystically
consist of sporadic static punctuated
by fragments of apparent lucidity.
It is the periods of silence, however,
which make the most sense.

The fourth, launch-date unknown,
will dispense with all transmissions. Being
the last of the series, it will be manned.

Honey

"...the point of travelling is not
to arrive, but to return home
laden with pollen you shall work up
into the honey the mind feeds on."

R. S. Thomas

                Mine
derives from many different flowers:
the scientific and comic; psychological
and aesthetic; spiritual and sexual;
with others, more rarely visited, which
still impart their own peculiar qualities.

It has at times a strange taste,
but my mind could not feed on that
from only one species; the purity
would kill me. And I like too much
the dance of the bees denoting
a fresh source.

Dancing the Ultra-Violet

The First Haiku of Spring

A wren sings her song
perched on the branch of a tree
in next-door's garden.

*

Blackbird on the lawn
cocks his head attentively.
A worm holds its breath.

*

A solitary
coal-tit's persistence pays off:
the prize is peanuts.

*

From the highest branch
a robin sings defiance.
We say: 'How cheerful!'

*

Trying to copy
the blue-tit's acrobatics,
a sparrow looks daft.

*

Bully-boy starlings
monopolise the bird-bath.
Nemesis stalks them.

*

Dab-of-red face and
sudden flashes of yellow:
goldfinch glittering.

The Flexible Liner

Horrendously heavy, the black roll of butyl
Buckles and slumps in the Garden Centre car-park,
Passively resists being stuffed in the boot:
Like a recalcitrant corpse.

Back home, is reluctant to quit the car,
Snuggles the spare tyre. Yanked out,
Flops to garage floor, lies inert:
Like a slumbering snake.

Unrolled, does not stay flat as knife begins
To slice, trim and shape. Yields suddenly,
Becomes surprisingly compliant:
Like a hypnotist's victim.

Stretched across embryonic pond, paving stones
To hold the edges down, water hose-piped in,
Starts distending, assumes the contours:
Like a pregnant belly.

Is now in place, edges covered in earth, hidden by flint.
Thin boundary between pond and not-pond;
Precondition of pond's existence:
Like an act of faith.

The Garden Pond (I)

From clumps of weed sticklebacks dart.
Tadpoles seethe and surge with flailing tail
While upside-down among them floats a snail.
A newt is crawling where the shallows start.
A lily leaf unfurls its dark-red heart;
Marsh-marigolds send forth a tangled trail
Of root and stem, which thrusting reeds impale.
A caterpillar's drowning in the deepest part.

This mini-universe is my creation.
I know its depths. I gave it love and life.
As I gaze, amazement and elation
Fill me, justify the sweat, the strife.
    Yet it knows me not. My shaping hand
    Is more than fish or weed can understand.

The Garden Pond (II)

The crystalline perfection of my pond
Has been disfigured by the unforeseen
Invasion of a sunlight-stealing green
And fuzzy growth, which fails to respond
To my attempts at clearing it. Beyond
Control, no quickly-fixable machine,
This pond cannot be forced to be pristine.
There is no cleansing spell or magic wand.

Within the murky water, snails lurk.
They welcome algae: this is food galore.
What I see menacing my handiwork
Is very snail heaven: give us more!
    The pond is theirs, whatever I contrive:
    Engulfed in green, they eat and breed and thrive.

Between Worlds

A patch of slender reeds.
Part-way up one blade,
A bug. Unprepossessing brown,
Misshapen-thumbnail-size.
Inhabitant, till now, of pond-sludge.

In the fabric of its back
A split, from which extrudes
An elongated mass,
A squeeze of greenish-yellow
From an oil-painter's tube.

Unrecognizable at first,
A twitch betrays identity:
Nascent dragonfly,
Gauze wings still pressed
To resurrection body.

She dangles like an escapologist
In mid-manoeuvre.
The realm of water
Has relinquished her,
Air has yet to claim her.

The dragonfly is resting
On the husk of former self.
She spreads her wings to dry.
Suddenly, is gone.
The six legs of the husk

Still clasp the reed tenaciously.

The Old Fence

The new fence is higher.
We cannot see into next-door's garden.

The new fence is stronger.
It does not wobble in the wind and has no creaking voice.

The new fence is longer.
Cat-sized holes do not punctuate its length.

Roses are not climbing the new fence.
Creepers are not creeping along its slats, nor ivy thriving.

Preservative preserves the new fence.
Tar is retarding any subsoil rotting of its posts.

The old fence has been broken up.

Cabbage White

Not very special-looking:
Flitting among the wild-flowers
On wings the shade of stale paper
Foxed with spots of mould.

Easy to dismiss you as dull
Compared to your glamorous cousins:
Emperor, Peacock, Painted Lady,
Whose gaiety so delights.

But give me eyes like yours –
Eyes that respond beyond
The human spectrum, eyes
That make the invisible visible –

Give me such butterfly eyes
And your wings will dazzle
With shimmering filigree,
And dance the ultra-violet.

Swallows

The swallows are swooping low today
Over the river's flat calm. Their incessant
Insect-seeking ways, their broken-crescent
Wings and pencilled-in tails display
The essence of a bird for which to play
Is to work and to be; and only the present
Is open to them, the evanescent
Moment. Ten years ago on New Year's Day
I watched such as these criss-cross the sky
Of Africa. Homesick for Devon, I felt
Their presence as a warmth within, to melt
My male pride, allowing me to cry.
Untroubled by the sense I make them bear,
The swallows soar and swoop and slice the air.

Detachment

Not a hint of a breeze this autumn morning
as smudges of thaw speckle the frosted fields
beneath an unclouded sun;

but from a slender birch
a leaf casually flutters down,
followed by a second, a third...

erratic tracks of mottled yellow,
occasional mini-cascades when
one leaf flicks another.

No computations involving gravity,
the Brownian motion of air molecules,
and seasonal variations in the viscosity of birch tree sap

could possibly predict
which will be the next leaf to fall,
or plot its track from twig to earth.

I stare at one leaf, willing it to be
the next metaphor for life's uncertainty.
It resists my will, remains tree-bound.

Waiting for Angels

In the presence of trees
even the gods are silent,
waiting for angels to settle
on branches charged
with green and vermilion.

The trees tolerate the gods
but do not acknowledge them,
allowing them to creep
into fissures in the bark
disguised as beetles.

When the angels are restless
the air sings
and the dark of the trees
gives way to elusive light
which only the half-closed eye discerns.

In the presence of trees
our mystery is comprehended
by root and branch and leaf,
of which the gods
are ignorant.

At Woodbury Castle

There are beech trees now at Woodbury Castle,
sliding down the earth banks,
husks and leaves strewn thickly in the ditch.
They jigsaw the sunlight,
green the air,
play host to fungi, moss, magpies, beetles.

Their columns calm the eye,
their branches catch the breeze,
the breathing of their leaves eludes the ear,
their roots... ah, their roots...
Their roots wriggle into leaf-mould,
into earth, into...

Eighty generations back came the Celts
who dig the ditches three men deep,
raise the ramparts two men high,
haul up timber for their huts,
fortify their hill-top home.
Now, they lord it over the land.

Grassland gives their cattle grazing;
the river teems with salmon, trout;
corn grows, the women bake their bread;
and sacrifices to their gods should bring
prosperity, protection, success in battle.
And here they live, and here they die...

Strollers stroll among the beech trees,
gaze across the Common,
take photographs.

Sonnet to the River Otter
(in response to S.T. Coleridge's poem of the same title)

Today you flow as placidly as on
The childhood days recalled by STC.
Your windings offer cheerful company,
Your waters welcome goose and gull and swan.
But recently you roared a different song,
Tried to drown a town, swirled sludgy
Shingle into shop and house, left misery.
Your charms concealed a temper all along.
What then of childhood? Your poet yearns
To be a *careless child* once more, as though
His youthful years knew only joy. Not so!
For anger, fear and sadness took their turns.
       I'll walk your bank with him, arm in arm,
       And see the turbulence beneath the calm.

The Quarry

I take a trampled track that leads
Through sturdy stalks of head-high corn
Which wave in wind like surfing sea.
Above, a buzzard slowly turns.

Faint at first, then louder, louder,
Grows a noise that grates the ear:
Chugga! Chugga! Chugga! Chugga!
Resounding through the rural air.

Mountainscapes of greyish-white
Where stone dice of a giant lie
Surrounded by the gougings-out
Of land by man's machinery.

Years ago I watched a friend
Who loves the grasp and grain of stone
Caress the contours, check the planes
Of one misshapen slab, begin

A task of transformation. Hammer,
Chisel, drill and months of sweat
Helped her shape the stone from former
Lump to lines of loveliness.

Human hand, human eye
Bring their beauty to the earth.
The buzzard swoops to snatch its prey.
The corn is cut for human mouth.

The Falcon Sonnets

"Life lives out of its own ground, and springs from its own source.
Therefore it lives without Why…"

Meister Eckhart

"We are the ashes of stars."

John Barrow / Frank Tipler

I

He gripped, ripped a grey, writhing mess.
Falcon with plundered prey: pigeon, caught
In flight, brought down to feed, a deed wrought
In sun-parched, -patched back-yard; and, yes,
Talons tore, brute beak gored still-living flesh
As feathers flurried, white breast-feathers sought
The air, fell there, soft as snow in autumn
Sun. Done, prey-pigeon ceased to thresh.
The falcon fed awhile, fed there; then, head
High, his dark-bright eyes ranged the yard,
Wings half-spread in readiness, black-barred
Tail charged for flight… No flight, instead
The wings unspread themselves, the fierce head fell
Afresh to pigeon flesh. He feasted well.

II

Feasted well, but how aware? What impels
His soar and glide, his stoop, his grip and rip;
What unfolding destiny, what strip
Or shard of sense his pigeon-killing tells?
He kills to eat, he eats to live – that spells
Itself; in doing thus he's in the grip
Himself of evolution's one-way trip.
But why? What purpose falcon-life indwells?
He gives, can give, no answer. Nor can I;
But marvel at the falcon's falconings
That witness: life from life's own well-head springs.
He lives to live – he lives without a Why.
And I from that same well-head have my source:
I live; I am; I need no other force.

III

Force, fierce force, caused life lost, cost all
For falcon's feed, his prey, grey pigeon killed:
Sky-snatched, down-dashed and gashed, life-blood spilled.
No chance, no choice; the weak go to the wall.
One life fulfilled, another thrust in thrall
To death, to death delivered, breath stilled.
Grey mess, flayed unpigeoned mess: when filled
With former life, death-willed? To life's call
Deaf? No! This bird from first heard, knew,
Became her word, own word, word fleshed, no less
Than falcon; full able to express, to yes
The spark within. Such self the falcon slew.
If life from life's own well-head springs, it seems
The well-head's also fed by darker streams.

IV

Darker streams of chaos that contend
With order as it labours to emerge,
Bitter streams of nothingness that surge
With ceaseless threats to bring about the end.
Yet since the universe began, the trend
Has ever been the same; the onward urge
For life spurred on by death's attendant scourge.
And from the tension of the two, transcending
Both, there comes the birth within the heart,
The genesis of every inward spark,
The imprint of *what is*, the stamp, the mark
Of being – that of which we are a part
However far we come. However far,
We never lose the mark of what we are.

V

We are the ashes and the heirs of stars.
They fashion our atoms at furious pitch.
Their energies lash into being the rich
Elemental array, till with spent reservoirs
They succumb to a star-death, and fling out afar
In a flaring display all their progeny which
Will condense over aeons, form planets that hitch
To a system and burgeon with life's repertoire.
All of us come from the stars: the pigeon,
The falcon, the writer of words and the reader,
The woman of science, the mightiest leader,
The killer, the crazy, the man of religion:
All of us come from the stars, and the spark
Of the stars in our soul will enlighten the dark.

Had We Your Gifts

The Logic of Whistling

"My day passes between logic, whistling, going for walks and being depressed."

Ludwig Wittgenstein in a letter to Bertrand Russell

Given that
If I go for a walk
And I whistle,
Then I am not being depressed;

And either
If I am being depressed
And I go for a walk,
Then I do not whistle;

Or
If I walk depressed
And I am being a whistle
Then I do not go;

It follows that
If I go for a whistle
And I depress a walk,
Then I am not being.

Therefore
Whistling, walking and
Not being depressed
Beat the living daylights
Out of logic.

Lacking the Latin

"I've never attempted to achieve my potential."
Peter Cook

A cap, a mac, a monotone were all
That you required to make us cry with laughter:
Ignoramus Pete, a pompous judge,
Wisty with his *Interesting Facts,*
Sir Arthur teaching ravens how to fly
In water, a foul-mouthed yob, a leaping nun.

Would-be copycats appeared, but none
Remotely had your speed of wit and all
Of us agreed, whenever you let fly
Another shaft, that in creating laughter
You were supreme. The outcome of these facts?
Success for life, so far as we could judge.

But we admirers soon became your judge
And jury. We wanted more and more. When none
Or very little came, and when the facts
Emerged of private grief – the booze, the all-
Too-common family rows, divorce – our laughter
Waned. Had Cookie been too smart, too fly?

A comic Icarus who'd tried to fly
Beyond himself? A genius who couldn't judge
The real range of his potential laughter?
We shook our heads, drank beer, discussed how none
Of us, had we your gifts, would let it all
Disintegrate... A waste... But facts are facts...

Yet when we come at last to face the facts
Of our own lives, of how we've let time fly
Pursuing gross fatuities and all
The trivia our better selves would judge
To be as batty as your leaping nun,
Your best response will be sardonic laughter.

Perhaps we too should now dismiss with laughter
Attempts to claim as scientific facts
Alleged potentials. What if we have none?
Or no more than a donkey or a fly?
Your miner, who aspired to be a judge
Had he the Latin, answers for us all.

Laughter is just laughter. A fly's a fly.
There are no other facts by which to judge
Our lives, or those of others. None at all.

Caravaggio's 'The Fortune-Teller'

The gaze between them takes the attention:
the pretty, round-faced lass with fine eye-brows,
the young fop in his plumed hat and finery.

She is the confident one; with her quiet smile
she knows she has captivated her client.
He, the innocent, hopes he has made a conquest.

But the action is really all in the hands:
tracing his fortune in the upturned palm
her fingers are also removing his ring.

We smile at the young woman's ingenuity,
at the foolishness of the young man;
and perceive only slowly, if at all,

our quiet complicity in deception.

Vincent's Chair with Pipe

An ordinary chair
of yellow wood
and a simple rush seat
standing on rough, reddish tiles.

A sturdy, trustworthy chair
which will not lull you to sleep,
nor quickly make your backside sore,
nor filch your loose change.

A solitary chair
on which lie a pipe and tobacco pouch:
sole tenant of the framed space.

*

Outside the canvassed moment, the chair
is repositioned on the tiles,
the pipe and baccy picked up;
a backside is firmly planted on it
as the artist lights up and moodily
surveys the still-wet painting

of his chair.

At 'The Art of Holy Russia'

(an exhibition of icons from Moscow)

Though I try to look through them
Into another world,
My gaze keeps bouncing off
The solemn Madonnas and Child,
Anatomically-suspect angels,
Po-faced patriarchs.

Whether it is Russia
I am unable to enter
Or the mediaeval world,
Or the aesthetics of blue and gold,
Or simply the holy life,
The distance feels too great.

These icons are not my icons.
During the time I spend with them
Beech trees are left unhugged,
Beethoven's Late Quartets unplayed,
The coastal path unwalked,
My cat unstroked.

If My Father Were to See the Work of Rachel Whiteread

What would he make of it,
this manifestation of what isn't there?

The aisles of negative bookshelves
voided of books;

the implacable grey of concreted space
beneath absent tables where absent pupils sit;

the whitewashed brick wall paralleled
by its plaster-cast complement.

I imagine his brow begin to furrow,
the tiny shake of the head he would give;

see him listening courteously
as I mutter about seeing the unseeable;

hear him give his verdict of
"Emperor's new clothes!"

I picture the artist herself
coming to visit us, bringing

her concrete and plaster
to cast the intricate space

between father and son.

Presto
(Beethoven's String Quartet in B flat, opus 130: 2nd movement)

We are in the presence of a young woman
teasing her lover as she dances around him
with quick, light steps. For two short minutes
we join her delight and his infatuation
as she pirouettes away from his grasp,
laughs her sweet laugh and blows him
magical kisses…

or perhaps
we find ourselves in a winter garden
where leaves lying brittle with frost
are summoned by a skittish wind to join
an impromptu ceilidh on the lawn,
and their mesmeric whirling briefly
stills our own…

or perhaps
we are aware only of the notes
tumbling out in wonderful profusion,
and leaves whirl, the young woman dances,
in a realm we visit unaware; so when,
days later, we catch ourselves smiling
unexpectedly, the reason eludes us.

Of Sheep and Goats

"… as the shepherd separates sheep from goats."
Matthew 25:32

Just who would want to be a sheep
with their stupid flock mentality,
their quick capitulation to cajoling,
their constant brainless baaing
and their predestined date with mint sauce?

No, give me goat-hood any day
to roam at will about the world,
ingest exotic substances (laundry, cardboard boxes),
express my real feelings with a head butt,
make it with the nannies…

I'll take my chance that there exists
a hircine heaven every bit as real as
the ovine paradise. But if, however, only
hircine hell awaits – well, it will at least
be free of all those bleating sheep.

The Second Part

"My work consists of two parts: the one presented here plus all that I have <u>not</u> written. And it is precisely this second part that is the important one..."
Ludwig Wittgenstein, alluding to his *Tractatus Logico-Philosophicus*

I have not written
to my former lover
to say how special she is
despite the disappearance of
our fun in bed.

I have not written
to my old school friends
to say how I think of them still with affection
despite our all being well on the road
to boring-old-fartdom.

I have not written
to the Sainsbury's check-out girl
who greets a thousand customers with a smile;
to the cellist whose tender phrasing of Bach
has conjured a preview of heaven.

Nor have I written
to the thrush that is tapping at snails in my garden,
to the hedgehog nocturnally snuffling through leaves,
to the rooks cawing over the carpark,
to the bacteria in my gut...

I have not written,
            I have not written...

I have not even written
to Ludwig himself
to tell him how, despite my understanding
precious little of his work 'presented here',
he has opened my eyes

to the second part.

In the Lines of Your Face

Christmas Card

Despite the note I scrawled in last year's card
("Hope to see you sometime in the coming year")
And the self-same sentiment from you, I fear
That Christmas once again has caught us off our guard.
Why do we find it, well, the word's not 'hard',
More like 'impossible' to engineer
Some kind of get-together? It needs a mere
Quick lifting of the phone and *blah, blah, blah*'d
Do the trick. But perhaps at heart we feel
That making contact would be dangerous?
That both of us have changed, and what was real
Has died; that we'd discover what's left for us
Is just this annual ritual of the past
Which even as I write is fading fast.

Which, even as I write, is fading fast:
The actual past? – or some 'golden era',
About as credible as a chimera,
Fashioned out of self-deceit and vast
Amounts of ignorance? Although the past
We think we have does to us appear a
Real, lived-through past, a closer, clearer
Study shows how often we re-cast
Experience to make it take the form
We want it to, and so we stretch and cut
And twist our lives to fit a so-called norm
Of our devising – or of others'. But
Does this mean what I recall as good
And happy is simply misery, misunderstood?

"And *happy* is simply *misery misunderstood?*"
Those words themselves are miserable enough!
Are just as much unjust towards the stuff
Of life as claiming that unalloyed good
Describes our early years of friendship. Could
The time between our meeting in that duff
School play, and that crazy evening (at a rough
Guess twenty years ago) in a Petts Wood
Pub which was our so-far final drink
Together – could that time be plotted as
A graph of friendship's fluctuations, I think
We'd see the kind of wavy line which has
'Erratic' as a label, the ups and downs
Needing one another like verbs and nouns.

Needing one another like verbs and nouns
(With you the verb, the do-er, mover, always
On the go; and me so often in a daze,
A noun, content to be, without an ounce
Of action in my make-up, getting bounce
And bustle from your presence), we'd amaze
Ourselves and others by the many ways
We managed to survive those ups and downs.
But then our paths diverged. We met and made
New friends. My noun found other verbs, your verb
Found other nouns – and that is how it's stayed.
With neither of us wanting to disturb
The balance, a get-together *is* debarred:
Despite the note I scrawled in last year's card.

Couple Therapy

On these chairs sit
two tight rolls of barbed wire.

Each complains of the other's
sharp and unyielding nature.

When they leave at the end of the hour
a few barbs remain

embedded in the cushions.

At the Sea

Old men walk their wives
Along the shoreline of their lives;
Forty years of hand-in-hand
Watching water thrash the sand.

On the cliff-top girls and youths
Dance their suppositious truths
To music played *fortissimo*.
They have not heard the waves below.

Brave for a Moment

"There was a disciple in Damascus called Ananias, and he had a vision..."
Acts 9:10

What? Him? Coming to Damascus? The news,
Though half-expected, still came as a shock
To everyone here who followed the Way:
That arrogant, fanatical, murderous man
Of Tarsus – the blood of Stephen, our brother,
Staining his hands – had now set his sights on us.

Dreading to think what would happen to us,
We secretly gathered. In the light of this news
Should we flee? Or go underground? A brother
Burst in, out-of-breath, distraught. Another big shock:
A light in the sky! A voice! The very man
Who threatened us struck blind by God on the way!

We all erupted with relief at the way
In which the living God protected us.
Then came the murmurs of dissent: "The man
Must think we're mugs," said one. "This so-called news
Is meant to make us drop our guard in shock."
"Heads down and hide," agreed a second brother.

"But if it's true, then we should call *him* brother,
And visit him," I ventured. "That's the way,
Perhaps, to help him through his state of shock?"
"You're mad!" they shouted. "Are you one of us
Or one of them? We mustn't trust the news;
It's suicide to even see the man."

That night I could not sleep. A blinded man
In need of help was haunting me. A brother?
I tried to make myself distrust the news,
To no avail. He seemed to be God's way
Of throwing down the gauntlet, requiring us
To act upon the gospel, despite the shock.

Brave for a moment, I went. I saw with shock
What God had wrought within this Tarsus man:
Gone was every vestige of his hate for us.
He guessed my doubt, hugged me as a brother,
Prayed for healing, was baptized. Was shown the way
To the synagogue; preached the Good News.

Shocking to think of Saul, now Paul, a brother.
Strange man. Forceful. Has to have his own way.
Travels a lot. At times, sends us his news.

Sophia

What of the woman who lives in the man
Waiting to be welcomed?

Borne in his blood, embedded in his bone,
Enfolded in the creases of his skin:

She searches out the pathways of his spirit,
Knows the secret places of his soul.

Her mouth forms words, each becomes itself;
Her ears hear mysteries, her nostrils
                              breathe in ecstasy.

The love of letting be shines in her eyes;
Her fingers touch and quicken all creation.

Such is the woman who lives in the man
Waiting to be welcomed.

Family Funeral

I

Unfamiliar territory, this:
Wine and buffet at his house;

Admiring his prize collection of silver somethings
Neatly arrayed in their wall-mounted display case;

Reliving our myths and histories
Mingled with news of children, grandchildren;

Feeling faintly amazed that this bizarre
Assemblage of human beings is family;

Recalling with a jolt that we're here
Because one of us is no longer here;

Guests of an unseen host, wondering
Which of us will host the next gathering.

II

His death is a fine white powder
Sprinkled on our web.

The strands between us show up
As still intact

Despite the years of battering from individual
Histories, geographies.

The twisting thread untwists, re-twists,
Extends the web.

To Solitude

Easier by far to find you on the river bank,
  Or in the middle of a wind-swept moor,
Or on an isolated headland overlooking
    An inaccessible shore,
  Than in the city centre, or railway booking
    Office or department store.
But the heart can fail at any time, the mind go blank
    When the clash and the clamour overwhelm
      Spirit and flesh,
    With every urgent voice a fresh
      And fiercer torture, and new
Suffocations pile on, page after diary page:
    Ah! The choking, inner rage!
    Then there is hunger in the heart for you
      And your realm.

    You are sea-breeze,
    You are mountain-spring,
  You are cool shade under spreading trees,
  You are rain that ends a year-long drought;
    Yours is the song to sing
    To revive a belief
  In the goodness of life, and quieten doubt.
  In your domain the grind and the grief
    Of the workaday
    World fall away.
  You are rest, you are relief.

But you are more than this! You offer more to life
   Than just a fleeting interlude between
         Strife and strife,
   A stretch of existential quarantine
      Protecting us from further ills,
A momentary respite from an endless din;
   You are not a mere escape-road
   For when we lose control and shed our load
   Negotiating one of life's steep hills –
         No, you are much more:
I have lately realised to you is owed
      The wealth that all our lives can mean;
            Goddess within,
            You are our core.

   I knew you many years ago: you came
   When I was a boy and lying in bed before sleep.
         Every night
   When my parents had kissed me, had put out the light
      And were sitting downstairs with the news,
         Then, little girl, you would creep,
         Shyly, behind my shut lids.
            Not knowing your name
               But entranced,
            I watched as you danced
         And wished I could do as you did.
   But soon a belief that boys should not think
      Of dressing and dancing in pink
         Began to confuse
         This dream-awake kid:
   I watched you no more when you danced in the night;
   I watched you no more – you faded from sight.

For years you could not speak with me:
I thought you some peculiarity
    I had outgrown;
    I made the choice
  To disregard your voice –
  I did not understand
    You are my own.
When, no longer as a little girl in pink
    But as a figure in maturity
    You made your powers known,
    I felt at first unmanned,
  And only as you called on me to drink
  The waters from the well-spring
        Of originality
    Which is yours alone,
Could I begin to comprehend and, comprehending,
        Rejoice.

  For I have heard you on the cello
  As you summon into being such tones
      Of anguished, mellow
Beauty as to make God weep. I have seen
    You sweating in the sculptor's studio
        Where the stone's
  Mass unmasks its hidden form
      To your persuasion.
      I have been
  By your side in the lab as a swarm
Of new particles yields to a new equation
    And new understanding is born.
      Muse and midwife
    To all creative life,
You are the midnight oil and the first streak of dawn.

I find you in my study at the desk
Thumbing through my note-books,
Reading all the half-heard phrases,
Scraps of jokes and vague ideas
    That fill the pages.
      It appears
You find them funny, sad, grotesque,
    Profound, peculiar, pointless…
But I must not disturb: I wait in terror and elation
      Until you discern
  A cadence scribbled in a pencilled mess
Of other jottings smudged to near obliteration.
      You turn.
    I know your looks.
    I see your eyes burn
With the fire of creation.
My heart quickens at your caress.

    I enter you.
    All sense of time suspended,
All the outside world now faded to a distant mist,
    Conscious solely of the one sensation,
      We alone exist.
    Our union is what we both intended
      For only, you insist,
Only full surrender will create the new,
Will bring to life the darling child of our imagination.

Someone is shouting my name
And hammering on the door:
    The world outside
Demands my presence once more.
    I must go, you say;
    I beg you to stay!
  We must hide! We must hide!
  But flickering like a dying flame
    You fade away.
  I am left to mourn,
Though your absence is not an absence of grace:
    For from our brief union a child
      Has been born.
      Our child,
  In the lines of whose face
    Is your face.

The Gap

TEN SPECULATIONS

on

Michelangelo's *The Creation of Adam*

On finger and finger
fierce charge accumulates.
Adam, God,
force-field between.
Across
      the fingered gap
crackles
an invisible spark.

The tensed forefinger
takes leave
of the other's languid hand.
God withdraws and
Adam is.
       The untouch
seethes between them.

In the almost
of not touching
Adam holds his breath:
one slip and
              annihilation
is assured. God's judgement
is perfect: His finger
tantalises.

Less than the width
of a proton or
greater than that
of the universe?
From finger-tip
to finger-tip
the distance between
God
        and Adam
is both.

Dare He stretch
the extra
however-much? How
might Adam respond
to the divine touch?
With derision or
delight? Is the risk
worth it?
        Like a lover
too nervous to
press the bell-push
God hesitates
while Adam waits.

With His finger
God pushes the gap
towards Adam,
tells him to take it
as gift
            and guarantee.
Not knowing what he's
meant to do
Adam keeps the gap
at arm's length.

One twitch from
Adam's finger
would complete
          the circuit,
would charge him as
fully with God
as God Himself.

A hammock slung
between Adam
                and God
belonging to neither but
needing them
both.

Fulcrum
of a see-saw
on which neither
God
    nor Adam
must rise too high
or fall too low.

A breathing space
for God and
a breathing space
for Adam
without which
both
        would suffocate.

Alas

"Alas, those verses one writes in youth aren't much. One should wait and gather sweetness and light all one's life... and then maybe at the end one might write ten good lines."

Rainer Maria Rilke

Abraham and God at the Gates of Sodom

Ten? Why ten? If at the end of life
I could put my name to nine of merit,
I'd surely be forgiven for lacking one;

And if nine suffice, why not eight, or seven?
Or even six? Six lines of such a sweetness,
Such refulgent light to set hearts dancing.

I could try five – or perhaps the ultimate quatrain;
But why risk ruining three exquisite lines?
Of course, a couplet has its virtues…

One good line would make me happy. One word.

Notes

Blizzard: Captain Oates was a member of Scott's 1910 expedition to the Antarctic. On their return journey he was crippled by frostbite and, fearing he was jeopardising his companions' chances of reaching safety, he walked out of the tent into the blizzard, commenting, "I am just going outside, and may be some time."

At Woodbury Castle: Woodbury Castle is the site of a prehistoric hill-fort on Woodbury Common in Devon. It originally had several lines of defence, and much of its main ditch and rampart is still evident. Excavations in 1971 suggest it dates to the first millennium BC, but the site was probably no longer used as a hill-fort after 300BC.

The Quarry: The hard chalky limestone from the quarry near Beer in Devon was used for some of the interior structure of Exeter Cathedral and for images on its West front. Sculptor Frances May also used it for her work *Trinity*, now located in the garden of the Bishop's Palace, Exeter.

Sonnet to the River Otter: The poet Samuel Taylor Coleridge (often known as STC) was born and brought up in Ottery St Mary, Devon, where his father was rector. He wrote his 'Sonnet to the River Otter' in 1793 when he was 21. By his own later admission his childhood was not as free of care as his poem implies: for example, when he was seven a furious argument resulted in STC going for his brother with a knife.

As for the river, on Thursday 7th August 1997 Ottery St Mary suffered a violent storm when, according to the next day's *Western Morning News*, "No less than three inches of rain – the normal amount for the whole of August – fell on the town during 45 terrifying minutes." Dozens of shops and houses were flooded, and one woman was "trapped in her home by the overflowing River Otter for more than two hours."

The Falcon Sonnets: Meister Eckhart (c.1260–c.1328) was a German mystic whose teachings, condemned by the church as heretical, went underground for centuries, re-emerged in the 19th century, and are currently enjoying a renaissance. See, for example,

Meister Eckhart: Selected Writings, selected and edited by Oliver Davies (Penguin, 1994); and my own *Echoes of Eckhart* (Arthur James Ltd, 1998).

The Barrow & Tipler quotation is from their book *The Anthropic Cosmological Principle* (Oxford, 1986).

Lacking the Latin: The quotation from the comedian Peter Cook (1937–95) was his response when accused on a TV chat show of not fulfilling his potential. The episode is recounted in *Peter Cook – A Biography* by Harry Thompson (Hodder & Stoughton, 1997). The title of the poem refers to Cook's inspired monologue in which, as a miner, he claims, "I could have been a judge only I didn't have the Latin. I didn't have the Latin for the judging." Other sketches alluded to include 'E. L. Wisty' droning on about allegedly interesting facts, the Leaping Nuns of the Order of St Vitus, and Cook's devastating parody of the judge in the Jeremy Thorpe trial.

If My Father Were to See the Work of Rachel Whiteread: Much of the work of Rachel Whiteread, who won the Turner Prize in 1993 with 'House', consists of plaster or concrete casts of spaces, such as the corridors between library book-shelves. An exhibition of her work was mounted at the Anthony d'Offay Gallery, London, in 1998–9.

At the Sea: I am indebted to Sue Lawrence for the opening image.